Applying The Business Model Canvas

A Practical Guide For Small Business

Design, Align, and Test Your Ideas

Steven Imke

Produced in the United States of America

First Printing, 2016

ISBN-13: 978-1533677983
ISBN-10: 1533677980

KSI Enterprises
395 Scrub Oak Circle
Monument CO 80132

www.SteveBizBlog.com

About the Author

Steve's first foray into the world of small business came when he was an Invisible Fencing dealer. He operated this business on a part-time basis while remaining employed by a Fortune 500 company called Digital Equipment Corporation (DEC). While the Invisible Fencing business was not very successful for Steve, it was a valuable opportunity for him to learn important lessons about business in a relatively low-risk environment.

After ending his relationship with Invisible Fencing, he worked on a business plan for a new business idea and waited for the right opportunity to present itself. In 1994, DEC fell on hard times. Instead of bemoaning this turbulent economic tide, Steve capitalized on this opportunity. He quit his day job at DEC to found Horizon Interactive, a documentation and training company. In fact, Horizon Interactive became a vendor for DEC.

Over the next few years, Steve and his partners executed the business plan. The business grew to over $3 million in annual sales and opened offices in several states. Horizon Interactive's success drew the attention of Interleaf, a publicly held company out of Massachusetts. In 1999, Interleaf acquired Horizon Interactive.

As part of the acquisition, Steve was offered the position of VP of Operations for their services division. Under his leadership, Interleaf acquired two more businesses like

Horizon Interactive. The company grew the services side of the business from a combined $8 million in revenue to over $32 million in sales during the next two years.

In 2001, Interleaf was acquired by Broadvision, a California company during the height of the dot com era. Broadvision primarily acquired Interleaf for their XML engineers who worked on the product side of the business. Needing to divest himself from the services business, Steve and a former business partner acquired the assets of Interleaf's service business and started IC Interactive. They operated the business for a few more years until they sold it in 2003.

Being a serial entrepreneur, Steve has started and still operates three different businesses. One of his businesses is focused on real estate. The second one is focused on oil and gas. His third business is a company designed to help high net-worth investors understand the ins and outs of investing in oil and gas direct participation programs.

Steve has volunteered his time since 2003 as a mentor for SCORE, a local organization dedicated to helping entrepreneurs. He has acted as their Chapter Chairman for several years. He is also an advisory board member of his local Small Business Development Center (SBDC). In additions to his advisory role, he also acts as a counselor for the SBDC since 2003. In 2012, Steve acted as the interim director of SBDC while they conducted a national search for a permanent director. Currently, Steve is the Entrepreneurship Director at Pikes Peak Community College and writes a daily blog about small businesses.

Steve is a flaming dyslexic, which has its good points and bad points. Growing up, he remembers undergoing a board of education evaluation. When asked to draw a tree, Steve drew a series of concentric rings. When asked about his drawing, he said the rings were what you see when you cut down the tree and look at the stump. These rings tell the entire life story of the tree. The evaluator told his parents he was not normal. He should be more like the other kids and draw the tree from the side view.

However, rather than conform to the crowd, Steve embraced his out-of-the-box thinking as an asset. The upside of being dyslexic is exceptional spatial awareness and problems solving skills. Dyslexics develop these heightened skills since they are forced from an early age to compensate for things they do not do well.

Being a dyslexic in school prevented Steve from becoming a good reader. Even today, spelling and grammar are not his strong suits. Academically, Steve struggled in traditional schools. When he graduated from high school, he knew that a traditional classroom education was not for him so he joined the United States Coast Guard to learn a trade. Graduating near the top of his class in tech school, Steve realized that he learned by doing.

Steve tends to be an overly logical person. He likes to explore, document, and measure nearly every aspect of a project to find out what works and what does not. He has a propensity to focus on understanding why things are the way they are rather than how to duplicate what others have already done. Once Steve obtains a reasonable level of mastery in a specific subject area, he internalizes the knowledge and moves on to his next area of interest.

Everything of substance Steve knows about small business initially began by him reading books, listening to audiobooks, or watching others. He internalizes the salient points, then rolls up his sleeves and puts them into practice in his own business. Once Steve perfects a lesson, he makes it a point to document it and then share it with others. He calls these "Sea Stories," leveraging his old Coast Guard days. In addition to sharing his knowledge, this practice serves to further solidify his learning in his own mind while continuing to grow his knowledge base. In this way, Steve has codified over more than a decade's worth of his small business knowledge in the various books he has written.

This process has served Steve pretty well. By the time he was 42 years old, Steve had reached the point where he no longer needed to work for money. Passing this income milestone has not only allowed him the luxury to spend even more time to ponder and digest life's lessons, but also the freedom to tell it like it is without the fear of losing his job. He proudly wears jeans nearly every day. He also sports facial hair to remind himself and others that being a nonconformist and not subscribing to traditional viewpoints has its merits for entrepreneurs.

Steve constantly reads and listens to non-fiction audiobooks about politics or business related topics. He consumes current events from a huge basket of news sources every day so he can relate their messages in new and innovative ways. After internalizing a message and testing new theories, he shares his new-found wisdom with people willing to listen.

Since 2003, Steve has mentored and counseled thousands of fledgling entrepreneurs through his volunteer efforts with SCORE and SBDC. He has volunteered his expertise to help organizations like ARC, a program which helps individuals with developmental disabilities.

As cliché as it may sound, Steve is at the point in his life where it is all about using his skills and knowledge to help others to succeed. Steve never expects anything in return, but simply enjoys the appreciation he receives from the people he has helped and lives vicariously through their success. For Steve, sharing his knowledge is akin to the feeling a billionaire might have handing out $100 bills to random strangers on the street. He knows that by sharing some of the wisdom he has accumulated with clients, he can often make a positive difference in their lives. Steve is not particularly religious so helping entrepreneurs is his way of giving back and making a significant impact on the world around him.

Table of Contents

Business Model Canvas 9 Blocks

The Business Model Canvas was proposed by <u>Alexander Osterwalder</u> and is based on his book, Business Model Ontology.

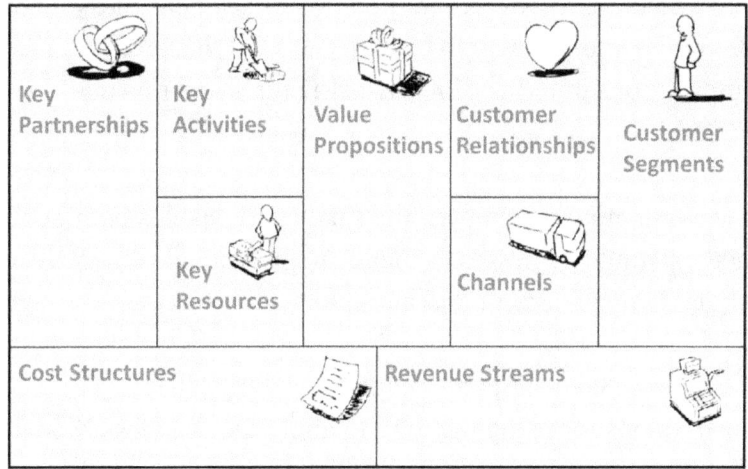

The Business Model Canvas is a strategic management and lean start-up template that a business can use when developing new or documenting existing business models. Basically, it is a visual representation that describes the nine critical elements of a firm's product or service offerings.

The Business Model Canvas assists the entrepreneur in aligning their activities by illustrating potential trade-offs. With the Business Model Canvas, a company can easily describe and present various business model conceptualizations to stake holders so they can be compared before marshaling the company's resources toward building and testing a minimally viable solution. Principally, the tool looks at the customer segments the product or service will target, the value proposition it will offer each customer, how it will reach them, the infrastructure it will require in terms of key activities, resources and partners to execute, and the financial implications in terms of its cost structures and revenue streams.

By completing the canvas, the final chart enables both new and existing businesses to focus on operational as well as strategic management and marketing.

I have created a simple template, including basic instructions for using the tool, to apply the Business Model Canvas to your business. This template is located in the "Resource" tab of SteveBizBlog.com.

In this eBook, we will look at the various blocks of the Business Model Canvas so you can better apply the tool to your specific situation.

Would your business benefit from utilizing the Business Model Canvas to capture the key elements of your business model in one graphical representation?

Customer Segments

Customer Segments

When creating a new Business Model Canvas, the first question any business must ask is "For whom are you creating value?" Sometimes that answer may be a bit complicated. For example, take PayPal. PayPal is an example of a multi-sided platform that connects both buyers and seller in a financial transaction. It essentially has two customers, each with a different value proposition.

Sometimes the customer may simply be a new segment of an existing market. Take for example Nike shoes. Nike initially targeted the runner which had a very specific set of needs as we discussed in the blog post titled, "Just Do It." However, Nike has expanded its line to included basketball, football, and baseball shoes as well. Each segment has its own set of value propositions.

A company may consider diversifying its customer offering. For example, General Motors developed robots to more efficiently assemble its automobiles. Since its robots could be used for other functions, General Motors sells its robots and technology to other companies. More specifically, my company created a series of training courses for a computer company that used General Motors' robots to assemble disk drives in a clean room environment.

Using the Business Model Canvas to lay out a visual representation for each customer segment is a great way to get a simple bird's eye view and give the entrepreneur the ability to assess which customer segment is the most important.

Do you have a clear picture of the customer segments your business targets?

Choosing a Customer Segment Type

The first step for a new business or an existing business coming out with a new product line is to define the customer segment they are targeting.

During the early stages of the process, I recommend starting out with a broad definition of the customer segment. The following is a list of five common customer segments types with a brief description to help you understand each of them.

Later in the planning process, you will have to put a finer point on the customer segment using demographics and psychographics, but during the early planning stages, all you need to consider is which one of the five broad customer segment types you will be targeting with your product or service.

1. **Mass Market** – You are making no distinction as to the audience of your product or service. Moreover, the value proposition will apply to all people. The iPod, iTunes, Blu-ray players, house painting, and dry cleaning are examples of a customer segment that appeals to the mass market with little or no differentiations.
2. **Niche Market** – In the old days before the internet and search engines, the only way to make money was to target the mass market. Today, businesses

can target very small segments of the market. For example, a manufacturer of replacement drone propellers is a niche market since it only applies to drown owners that are looking for a replacement propeller. Today, businesses can target them very accurately.

3. **Segmented** – You have one customer, but you can offer different value propositions or customer relationships. For example, consider banking. Banks have standard and private banking relationships with their customers. An individual may be the bank's consumer, but with private banking the customer relationship and value proposition is different. In private banking, the customer has a different customer relationship with the bank and is assigned an account person they can call for all issues. Additionally, the have a different value proposition as many services that have a fee, such as wiring money, are provided free of charge to private banking clients. While the bank may serve the same customer, there may be multiple ways they want to segment them with respect to the services offered. Moreover, many companies offer different services for subscribers vs. non-subscribers.

4. **Diversified** – You have one business model, but it serves two unrelated customer segments. For example, Wilson Sporting Goods sells sporting goods. One customer might be a football player. People who play football generally are young men. Wilson Sporting Goods also sells tennis equipment.

Tennis players are generally older and can be both male and female. As you can see, Wilson Sporting Goods has the same business model, but two very different customers.

5. **Multi-Sided** – You serve two independent customers related by your product or service. For example, credit card companies have two types of customers: merchants and card holders. Their business model addresses both of these customers, but with different sides of the same platform. Consignment shops and eBay are another good example of multi-sided customer segments as they serve both buyers and sellers with a single product/service.

What customer segment are you serving?

Serving Economic and End User Customer Segments

When fleshing out your business model canvas, you need to define your customer segment and value proposition. However, it is sometimes necessary to consider both the economic buyer and the end user when defining your customer segments.

For example, the other day I took my grandson to a Chuck-e-Cheese. The end user was my grandson and any value proposition for his customer segment would have to include providing a wide array of arcade style games for children of various age groups. Moreover, the value proposition would need to incorporate the child's desire to secure as many reward tickets as possible so that they could be exchanged for prizes and toys at the end of the visit.

But of course my grandson's customer segment would never have the means to show up or buy the tokens necessary to play the games. Therefore, Chuck-e-Cheese has a diversified customer segment and needs to account for the economic buyer (a.k.a. the adult) as well as the end user. To address this group, Chuck-e-Cheese offers the economic buyer security measures to make sure kids cannot leave the premises without physically being with the adult who brought them in. Additionally, Chuck-e-Cheese provides beer for the adults because we all know you have to have beer with pizza.

Does your value proposition address the needs of both the economic and end users of your customer segment?

Understanding Customer Segment Jobs

Once you have a good idea of your target customer segment, it is time to dig a little deeper. To do this, describe the specific tasks your customer segment is trying to do in their core job, the problems they are trying to solve, or the needs they are trying to satisfy.

Besides the customer segment's core job responsibilities, your customers may also be trying to look good in the eyes of another, gain status, or even secure more power for themselves. Perhaps your customers are looking for more security or to just feel better about themselves.

When examining the traits of your customer segment, you have to think outside their core responsibilities. To help put a finer point on the job of your customer segment, you can ask the following questions.

- What functions are you trying to help your customers perform? Are they trying to complete a task, solve a problem, or fulfill a need?
- What social needs are you trying to help your customers perform? Are you trying to help them look good, raise their status, or gain additional power?
- What emotional needs are you trying to help your customers perform? Are you trying to make them feel better about themselves or provide more

security?

After answering these questions, attempt to rank your customer segment's tasks, problems, and needs according to their significance, critical nature, and frequency. Finally, try to outline the context of their job to determine if there are any limitations or constraints that may apply.

Have you defined the tasks, problems, and needs of your customer segment?

Understanding Customer Segment Pain Points

Once you have a pretty good idea of the job your customer segment has to do, it is time to ferret out and define their pain points.

You can use the following questions to more accurately describe the customer's negative emotions, undesirable costs and situations, and risks they experience before, during, and after their job.

- What takes too long, costs too much, or requires too much effort in your customer's opinion?
- What frustrates, annoys, or gives your customer a headache?
- How are the current solutions under-performing for your customer? For example, is there a lack of features or low performance? Are other solutions prone to malfunctions or errors?
- What are the main difficulties or challenges your customer encounters? For example, do they have difficulty understanding how things actually work or get done?
- What negative social consequences could your customer encounter? For example, what causes your customer to lose face, power, trust, or status?
- Are there financial, social, or technical risks that your customer fears?

- Are there big issues, concerns, or worries that keeps your customer up at night?
- What are the common mistakes that your customer makes?
- Finally, what barriers keep your customer from adopting a solution? For example, are upfront costs too high? Are learning curves too lengthy? Does the customer resist change?

After answering these questions, attempt to rank your customer's pain points according to their significance and frequency.

Have you defined your costumer's pain points?

Understanding Customer Segment Gain Points

Once you have a pretty good idea of the job your customer segment has to do, it is time to ferret out and define their gain points. Use the following questions to describe the benefits your customer expects, desires, or would be surprised to receive.

- What savings in terms of time, money, or effort would make your customer happy?
- What outcomes in terms of quality and quantity does your customer expect? What would go beyond their expectations?
- What current features, performance, and quality items delight your customer?
- What would make your customer's job or life easier? For example, would a flatter learning curve, more options or services, or lower cost of ownership make your customer's life easier?
- What would make your customer look better in the eyes of others, increase their power, or raise their status?
- Is your customer looking for a better design, guarantees, specific features, or more features?
- Does your customer dream of big achievements or being relieved of burdens they have?
- How does your customer measure success? For example, do they measure success in terms of time,

cost, or performance?

- Finally, what would increase the likelihood that the customer would adopt a new solution? For example, would lower costs, risks, or investments better entice your customer? What about better quality or performance?

-

After answering these questions, attempt to rank your customer's gain points according to their significance and frequency.

Have you defined your customer's gain points?

Value Propositions

The second step in creating your Business Model Canvas is to identify your value proposition.

What is a value proposition? Simply put, a value proposition is a collection of products and services a business offers to meet the needs of its customers that helps to differentiate it from its competitors.

For example, several manufactures offer basketball shoes. However, playing basketball requires that the shoe fit tightly and provide good ankle support. To that end, Nike designed a shoe with small air chambers and a pump built into the tongue so that once the shoe was laced up the player could use the pump to fill the air chambers and create a tighter fit. In the end, Nike created a new product with a unique value proposition for a specific customer segment.

When completing the Business Model Canvas, you need to look at the specific customer segment identified earlier and answer the following questions:

- What value do you deliver to the customer?
- Which one of your customers' problems are you helping to solve?

- What bundles of products or services are you offering to each customer segment?
- Which customer needs are you satisfying?

The value proposition many be quantitative in nature such as lower price or higher efficiency or qualitative in nature such as providing an overall better customer experience or outcome.

Some specific examples of a value proposition you might provide as part of your differentiation might include:

- Better performance – as is the case with many new cars
- The ability to customize the solution to their specific needs – as is the case with many software applications
- Improved usability – such as error catching like a spell checker
- A better design – as with the Dyson vacuum

Do you have a clear picture of your value proposition for each of your customer segments?

Choosing a Value Proposition Type

When considering your unique value proposition, I find it helpful to consider a list of common value propositions to help guide me and my client's thinking. To that end, here are eleven common value propositions that businesses might offer to their selected customer segment. Review the following value proposition types and determine which one is most appropriate for your offering:

1. **New** – You have a new product or service unlike any other. Generally, your innovation is protected by a patent or something proprietary. When Invisible Fencing came out, they were the only product designed to contain a customer's dog based on the use of a radio transmitter, a perimeter wire, and a receiver collar worn by the dog.

2. **Performance** – PC manufactures generally deploy a new model that is faster and more powerful every 6 months to make the last version obsolete, encouraging the customer to upgrade. Car manufactures also produce new version each year that are a little more powerful and get better gas mileage.

3. **Customization** – 3D scanners, CAD programs, and 3D printers allow consumers to customize their final products. Many products (from software to cell phones) allow the user to customize the final

product to capture their unique personality or usage through customization.

4. **Get the Job Done** – When a person buys a condo, it often includes dues that cover all landscaping and exterior maintenance, relieving the consumer from this responsibility. If you offer a product or service that relieves the customer of some task they typically have to perform, you are providing a value proposition of getting the job done.

5. **Design** – The Dyson vacuum's value proposition uses a revolutionary bag-less design as a point of differentiation. While the vacuum cleaner itself was not a new product, it used a different design to capture market share. A design value proposition might also involve better ergonomics or just look cooler.

6. **Brand/Status** – The first generation of Cadillac Escalade was essentially a Chevy Tahoe rebadged to capture the status of Cadillac and thereby a higher margin associated with the prestige of Cadillac ownership. Name brands by virtue of their name often capture higher margins. For instance, Advil costs more than the generic equivalent, Ibuprofen.

7. **Price** – Southwest Airlines and Walmart have a low price value proposition. All activities are optimized to provide a low cost product.

8. **Cost Reduction** – Applications that operate in the Cloud, such as SalesForce, relieve the customer of the cost of buying, installing, and maintaining the application in exchange for a small subscription fee

as a way to reduce the customer's cost. Equipment rental/leasing companies are another example of businesses that offer a cost reduction value proposition. This type of company is especially valued by small, low duty cycle users to avoid the overhead and cost associated with physical ownership.

9. **Risk Reduction** – Offering an extended service guarantee is an example of risk reduction. When most car companies were offering a two year, twenty four thousand mile warranty, Chrysler offered a seven year, seventy thousand mile power train warranty, which was unheard of at the time. By extending the warranty, Chrysler reduced the customer's risk of owning a Chrysler product.

10. **Accessibility** – Most people can't afford a vacation home. However, with the advent of timeshares that offer the consumer a fractional ownership in a vacation property, ordinary people were provided access to vacation properties previously not available to them. Fractional ownership provides access to everything from airplanes to sailboats. Even the creation of mutual funds allowed the common person to have a diversified portfolio at a lower price point.

11. **Convenience/Usability** – When the iPod was introduced along with iTunes, it allowed busy users to search for music from a huge online library, download it, and listen to it all in a few minutes without ever leaving the comfort of their living

room. By offering this service, Apple provided unprecedented convenience and usability to their customers.

What value proposition do you offer to your customers?

Defining Your Value Proposition's Products and Services

After you understand the job, pain points, and gain points of your customers, it is time to define a value proposition to deliver to them. The products or services that you will provide can come in four different favors:

1. **Tangible** (e.g., manufactured goods or services delivered in person or face to face)
2. **Virtual** (e.g., downloads or online recommendations)
3. **Intangible** (e.g., copyrights or quality assurances)
4. **Financial** (e.g., investment funds or other financial services)

With these flavors in mind, make a list of all the products and services your company could deliver. Keep in mind the previous lists that you have made. For instance, consider the tasks, problems, and needs of your customer's job. Make sure to factor in how you ranked their significance, critical nature, and frequency.

Also consider the pain and gain points of your customer segment and how you ranked each point in terms of significance and frequency.

While you should consider all of these factors, it is now time to prioritize and focus on the key ones that you have the ability to deliver on as part of your solution.

Do you have a list of value propositions that you can test on your target customer segments?

Testing Your Value Proposition's Ability to Alleviate Pain

Now that you have a list of potential products or services that you plan to incorporate as part of your value proposition, you need to exposed them to the first test.

You can use the following questions to test your value proposition's products and services. These questions will help you determine if your products or services can alleviate the customer's pain points that they experience either before, during, and after performing their job.

Does your value proposition's products and services:
- Produce savings in terms of time, money, or effort?
- Eliminate your customer's frustrations, annoyances, and things that give him a headache?
- Provide new features, provide better performance, or quality that fixes under-performing solutions that currently exist?
- Remove negative social consequences such as loss of face, power, status, or trust?
- Eliminate your customer's financial, social, and technical risks/fears?
- Help your customer with his big issues, diminish his concerns, or eliminate some of his worries so he can sleep better at night?
- Help to eliminate mistakes or errors?

- Provide ways to remove the barriers that are keeping your customer from adopting a new solution such as lowering up-front investment costs, flattening the learning curve, or offering less resistance to change?

Do the products and services of your value proposition relieve your customer's pain?

Testing Your Value Proposition's Ability to Deliver Gains

Now that you have a potential list of products or services that you plan to incorporate as part of your value proposition, you need to see if it creates the benefits your customer expects, desires, or would be surprised to see.

You can use the following questions to test your value proposition's products and services to see if they will create customer gains before, during, and after your customers perform their job.

Does your value proposition's products and services:
- Create savings in terms of time, money, and effort that will make your customer happy?
- Produce the outcomes your customer expects or go beyond their expectations in terms of quality and quantity?
- Copy or out-perform current solutions that delight your customer in terms of more features, specific features, performance, or quality?
- Make the customer's job easier in terms of a flatter learning curve, better accessibility, more services, or lower cost of ownership?
- Create positive social consequences that your customer desires such as making them look better in the eyes of others, increase power, or raise status?
- Do something that your customer has been looking

for such as providing a better design, guarantee, more features, or specific features?

- Fulfill something your customer is dreaming about such as a big achievement?
- Produce positive outcomes that match your customer's success or failure criteria?
- Provide ways that you can help them make adoption easier such as lowering up-front investment costs, flattening the learning curve, or offering less resistance to change?

Do your products and services create customer gains?

Testing Your Customer Segment and Value Proposition Hypothesis

Once you have made a hypothesis regarding your customer segment and value proposition, you need to gather insight to validate your hypothesis by designing questions or experiments to take to potential customers.

If you are designing questions, it is important to avoid questions that will influence the customer's response. In other words, avoid leading questions or questions that ask for an opinion. For example you would NOT want to say, "Would you pay for X?" Rather ask, "When was the last time you paid for X?" The second question is far less subjective and leading.

Remember that you are not trying to get recognition for your idea. Rather you are trying to gain a deeper understanding of your customer segment by collecting evidence. This evidence will then determine if your hypothesis is correct or if you need to pivot.

You can ask your questions either in person, face to face, or even over the phone. However, while you can use questions to validate and test your value proposition, the best tests involve actual experiments with a call to action to see how a customer will actually respond to your value proposition.

For example, you could use a fake three page website. The

first page is a long form sales page that lists everything the customer needs to know to buy your product. The second page collects the buyer payment information. Finally, the last page says something like "out of stock" and "check back later." Experiments that closely mimic what you want the customer segment to do will provide the best evidence that you are on track.

Do you validate your value proposition by testing your customer segments?

Channels

When we refer to channels in the Business Model Canvas, we are speaking about marketing channels or distribution channels.

What exactly are these channels? Essentially, a channel is the way products and services get to the consumer.

With respect to the Business Model Canvas, it is a specific set of five practices or activities your business will use to transfer the ownership of goods from the point of production to the point of consumption. When it comes to examining the channels your business will use, we must consider how it will handle each of five phases.

1. How will you raise the **awareness** about the company and its products and services? For example, will you advertise on TV, go to trade shows, or engage in social media?

2. How will you help customers **evaluate** the organization's complete value proposition? For example, does it involve educating the customers or third parties about your offerings?

3. How will you allow customers to **purchase** specific products and services? For example, will you sell directly to the consumer through a website or

storefront or will it be indirect and involve distributors or affiliates?

4. How will you **deliver** the value proposition to customers? For example, will it be by providing a product or service that fits their specified needs better or will it be through better or more convenient hours of operations?

5. How will you provide post-purchase **customer support**? For example, will you offer a guarantee or warranty or will you provide technical support?

Collectively, when it comes to identifying the channels you will use, you also need to understand if you can integrate these channels with others you have already established, assess which ones will work best, and identify which ones are more cost efficient for you to implement.

Do you have a clear picture of the channels you use to reach each of your customer segments?

Customer Relationships

When it comes to customer relationships within the framework of the Business Model Canvas, we are talking about the ways that you will interact with each customer segment.

What type of relationship does each of your customer segments expect you to establish and maintain with them?

- Do they demand technical assistance and hand holding during the sales process such as the **face-to-face** interaction you receive when you buy a new car or home?
- Will a person on a **phone** and able to answer questions and handle their order such as when you order a new pair of shoes from Zappos be ok?
- Perhaps they expect an **automated system**, such as a website like Amazon, that remembers your past orders and offers recommendations or Dell, where you can customize and build a new desktop computer.
- Perhaps they expect a **self-service** relationship such as a simple e-commerce site or a WalMart experience.

Collectively, when it comes to identifying the customer relationship you will use, you need to also understand:

- Which ones you have already established?
- How can they be integrated with the rest of our business model?
- How costly are they are to implement and maintain?

When we talk about integration, we are really talking about the back-end systems you will use for managing your company's interactions with your current and future customers. Integration often involves using technology such as Customer Relations Management (CRM) software to organize, automate, and synchronize sales, marketing, customer service, and technical support.

Do you have a clear picture of the customer relationships each customer segment expects you to establish and maintain with them?

Choosing a Customer Relationship Type

The type of customer relationship that is right for your business depends on your customer acquisition costs, customer retention goals, and need to up-sell the customer on add-on or related products in the future. When considering different customer relationship types, I find it helpful to consider a list of common customer relationships to guide me and my client's thinking. To that end, here are six common customer relationship types that most businesses might offer to their selected customer segment. Review the following common customer relationship types and determine which one is most appropriate for your offering:

1. **Personal Assistant** – When you buy a new suit or a new car, you rely on a salesperson to show off the product's features and benefits. In this case, a personal assistant (frequently called a salesman or saleswoman) who has no long-term connection with the customer after the sale is an appropriate customer relationship type.

2. **Dedicated Personal Assistant** – At my bank, I have a private banking relationship where a specific and dedicated banker is assigned to my banking and investment relationship. In many businesses, a customer is assigned to a dedicated account manager who is familiar with the customer and manages the relationship.

3. **Self Service** – Most supermarkets are a good example of a self service customer relationship where you as a consumer are left to your own devices to locate the product and make your purchasing decisions without any assistance from the business.

4. **Automated Service** – Amazon is an example of an automated service where an application makes recommendations based on previous purchases and upon what similar buyers looked at or purchased. Another example that comes to mind is LinkedIn. LinkedIn helps you make connections by asking you "Do you know these people?" The key to an automated service comes from the ability to make recommendations for you.

5. **Communities** – I used to use the Avid video editing tool that relied on a user community to provide support. When I was having a problem I could not solve myself, I went to a message board and either searched the database for an answer or posed the question to the community of users and checked back later to see if I got any responses. Community customer relationships rely on non-company users to remain actively engaged.

6. **Co-Creation** – YouTube is an good example of a customer relationship that uses co-creation because it relies on its user base to create content. Co-creation businesses invite their users to be part of the process, such as when Amazon encourages

customers to write reviews about products they bought on the Amazon.com.

What customer relationship does your business use?

Revenue Streams

When it comes to revenue streams as part of the overall Business Model Canvas, there are may factors that effect the sources of revenue.

First, we must consider the fixed or list price of your product or service. However, when it comes to defining pricing you have several options:

- Do you offer **discount pricing** if they buy in bulk.
- Do you offer **variable pricing** based on the customer segment? For example senior or military pricing.
- Perhaps your revenue stream may come through **negotiated pricing** such as when you buy a car or home.
- Perhaps your revenue is involves **performance driven pricing** such as with a realtor's commission or a financial adviser being paid based on a portfolio's value.
- Or maybe it is based on **real-time market pricing** such as selling a commodity like crude oil.

When it comes to revenue streams as part of the overall Business Model Canvas development process, we are also talking about the other ways you have to separate your customers from their money. We have affectionately referred to these ways as your <u>Revenue Drivers</u>.

In addition to the actual fixed price revenue you might receive for selling a product or delivering a service, there are a bunch of other sources of incomes you can generate through the use of various fees. Some common examples might include:

- usage fees
- subscriptions fees
- royalty fees
- rental or leasing fees
- licensing fees
- financing fees
- brokerage fees
- advertising fees

When looking at your revenue streams, you have to consider the following questions:
- For what value are your customers really willing to pay?
- What do they currently pay?
- How are they currently paying?
- How would they prefer to pay?
- How much does each revenue stream contribute to your overall business revenues?

When it comes to your revenue streams, do you have a clear picture of all the ways you will generate revenue?

Choosing a Revenue Stream

When it comes revenue streams, they are generally either **"transactional,"** resulting from a one-time payment, or **"recurring,"** resulting from ongoing payments that deliver value or provide post-sales support. When it comes to defining a business's revenue streams, I find it helpful to consider a list of different types of revenue streams to guide me and my client's thinking. To that end, here are seven common revenue streams that many businesses might receive for their selected customer segment. Review the following common types of revenue streams and determine which one is most appropriate for your offering:

1. **Asset Sale** – This type of revenue stream is where someone sells ownership of a physical asset, such as a car or furniture. Once owned by the consumer, he is free to do with it as he chooses. He can use it or sell it without permission from the producer of the product. Asset sales are transactional revenue.

2. **Usage Fees** – The more it is used, the more the customer pays the company. When you book a hotel room, you pay based on the number of nights you stay, which is a usage fee. You never own the room, but are simply granted permission to use it for a period of time. A cell phone's data plan is another example. For cell phone data plans, the wireless carrier charges the customer a usage fee based on the data used. Usage fees are recurring revenue.

3. **Subscription Fees** – Revenue is generated by continuing to provide access to a service. Fitness centers have a monthly subscription plan to continue to provide the user access to the gym. Netflix charges a monthly subscription fee to provide continued access to its online streaming video service. With a subscription fee, the user is granted unlimited access to the service during the subscription period. Subscription fees are recurring revenue.

4. **Lending/Renting/Leasing** – Revenue is generated by temporally granting exclusive rights to use an asset for a fixed period of time. When you rent a car, the rental agency gives you exclusive use of the vehicle for the term of the rental agreement. No one else can use the asset while it is assigned to the customer. However, once the period is over, the asset can be assigned to another customer and the customer has no ownership of the product during the term besides the exclusive right to use it. Lending, renting, and leasing can be either transactional or recurring revenue.

5. **Licensing** – Revenue is generated by giving the customer permission to use protected intellectual property and allowing the customer the right to generate revenue from the property. Patent holders often license their ideas to a manufacture in exchange for a fixed fee or a royalty on all sales. Licensing can be either transactional or recurring revenue.

6. **Brokerage Fees** – Revenue is generated by an intermediary service performed between two or more parties. A credit card company collects a brokerage fee by connecting the merchant to the customer. The credit card company owns nothing and just facilitates the transaction. Another example of a brokerage fee is when a real estate broker captures a commission at the closing of a sell for matching buyers and sellers. Brokerage fees are typically transactional revenue.

7. **Advertising** – Revenue is generated from fees charged to a third party to present a message to your customers. Advertising can be either transactional or recurring revenue.

What revenue stream does your business use?

Understanding Pricing Mechanisms

Pricing mechanisms come in two principle forms: fixed and dynamic. **Fixed** pricing has predefined prices based on a static set of variables while **dynamic** pricing changes prices based on market conditions. Price mechanisms can effect both your revenue stream as well as your costs. When it comes to defining a business's pricing mechanism, I find it helpful to consider a list of different types of pricing mechanisms to guide me and my client's thinking. To that end, here are some common pricing mechanisms that many businesses might use for their selected customer segment. Review the following common types of pricing mechanisms and determine which one is most appropriate for your offering:

Fixed Pricing

- **List Price** – A fixed price for products or services is assigned. A good example is the prices associated with various meal choices at a restaurant.
- **Product Feature Dependent** – The price depends upon the quality or value proposition features. For example, when you buy meat at the butcher, you have a choice of cuts based on the USDA grading system that included prime, choice, or select cuts of meat. Another example of product feature dependent pricing is where the customer is charged a different rate based on when it is used. Cruise ship companies have different prices to book the same

stateroom during peak times, shoulder times, and off peak times.
- **Customer Segment Dependent** – The price depends on the type and characteristic of the customer segment. For example, many businesses offer special discounted rates for veterans or seniors.
- **Volume Dependent** – The price charged is a function of quantity purchased. For example, VistaPrint charges $7.10 for 100 basic business cards and $8.50 for 500.

Dynamic Pricing
- **Negotiated Pricing** – The price a customer pays is based on a negotiated price conducted between two or more partners. The price a customer pays is dependent upon the strength of his negotiation position as well as his negotiation skills. When you buy a car, the buyer and seller negotiate the final price of the vehicle.
- **Yield Management** – The price a customer pays is dependent on inventory at the time of purchase. A good example of yield management pricing is the price a customer pays for an airline ticket or hotel room. Based on the inventory of available seats or beds compared to an expected quantity, the price can go up or down to maximize the company's margins.

- **Real-Time Market** – The price is established dynamically based on broader supply and demand issues. For example, the price of a stock rises and falls based on the number of buyers and sellers at any given time who are interested in buying or selling the underlining stock. Commodities like eggs or crude oil are another example of real-time market pricing that vary based on supply and demand issues.
- **Auction** – The price is determined by the outcome of a competitive bidding process. Whether at an estate sale or on eBay, the final price of a product is determined through an auction process.

What pricing mechanisms does your business use?

Key Resources

For a company to produce a product or service, it needs access to:

- physical resources
- intellectual resources
- human resources
- financial resources.

Depending upon the value proposition defined in your Business Model Canvas, you will require more of one resource and less of another. For example, a manufacturing company requires physical resources in terms of machines as well as financial resources to buy raw materials and carry inventory. By contrast, a design company requires more intellectual and human resources.

Physical resources include such things as:

- buildings
- vehicles
- machines
- point-of-sales systems
- distribution networks.

Large retailers like Wal-Mart and manufacturing facilities rely heavily on physical resources which are often also very capital-intensive.

Intellectual resources include such things as:

- brands
- proprietary knowledge
- patents and copyrights
- partnerships
- customer databases.

Intellectual resources often take time to develop. Some companies like Nike and Sony rely heavily on their brands.

Some companies rely on **proprietary knowledge**. Unlike copyrights or patents, proprietary knowledge never expires. Some example include a secret formula such as for Bush's Baked Beans or Kentucky Fried Chicken's 11 herds and spices. Proprietary knowledge may include trade secrets like Google's search engine algorithm. Other times proprietary knowledge can come in the form of licensed materials. Companies like Walt Disney generate a large share of their revenue by licensing its characters to manufactures.

Next, enterprises need **human resources**, but those resources are particularly prominent in knowledge-intensive and creative industries. A pharmaceutical company relies heavily on human resources such as it's skilled scientists and aggressive sales force.

Finally, some business models depend heavily on **financial resources**. For example, cell phone companies that finance the consumer's phone purchases across a 2-year contract period rely heavily on financial resources.

When considering key resources, you must consider which key resources your value proposition requires.

- What key resources do your distribution channels require?
- What key resources do your customer relations require?
- What key resources do your revenue streams require?

When it comes to your key resources, do you have a clear picture of the degree to which your offering relies on each of the four key resource types?

Key Activities

Key Activities

When it comes to the Business Model Canvas, key activities are any activities that your business is engaged in for the primary purpose of making a profit.

Business activities include:

- operations
- marketing
- production
- problem solving
- administration

The key activities a business performs can be divided into four subsystems:

- core
- support
- coordination
- strategic

Core activities are tasks that are directly related to the the generation of its output such as manufacturing, assembly, or service delivery.

Next, **support** activities are tasks that support the production of outputs, but do not directly cause them to be generated such as record keeping, email, and training.

Then, there are **coordination** activities that are tasks that help to coordinate, develop, or integrate activities within and between core and support activities. Some examples are billing, forecasting, and account management.

Finally, there are **strategic** activities that link the outside environment and assess the degree of alignment and need for change such as marketing and sales.

When considering key activities, you must consider the following questions:

- What key activities do your value propositions require?
- What key activities do your distribution channels require?
- What key activities do your customer relationships require?

Key activities are ongoing and are focused on creating value for shareholders.

Do you have a clear picture of all the key activities you have to perform to produce your output?

Key Partners

Most companies are simply a link in a much larger value chain. We often think of our customers as terminal users of our products and services, but in reality our customers are most often simply the next link in the chain.

When it comes to the Business Model Canvas, the companies that supply you with products and services or receive your output, but are not the terminal users of your product or service, are consider your key partners.

There is a bit of a distinction that can be made between a simple supplier and a true partner.

A **supplier** is a company that you choose to provide a needed product or service and is more of a commodity-based provider. Communications with suppliers are primarily one way and they can be easily replaced with another supplier if needed.

A **partner** can be a key upstream supplier or downstream customer that has a greater interest in your success. Partners are more engaged in your process and help you provide a better product or service.

Your key partners are often chosen to optimize expensive

capital resources through their economies of scale. For example, a general contractor is often better served by outsourcing their dirt work to a dirt work contractor. Owning their own excavator is not very efficient based on a lower duty cycle of the asset.

Sometimes key partners are chosen to mitigate risk and uncertainty by transferring it to a partner who is in a better position to handle them. Such was the case with banks that sold their mortgages to Fannie Mae and Freddie Mac which sorted them by risk and sold them as mortgage-backed securities.

Finally, key partners may be chosen based on their unique set of resources or activities such as when Dodge chose to manufacture diesel trucks with the Cummins engine.

When considering key partners, you must first consider the following question:

- Who are your key partners and who are your suppliers?
- Next, you must consider which key resources you are acquiring from key partners and suppliers.
- Finally, what key activities do your key partners and suppliers perform?

Do you know who your key partners are?

Cost Structure

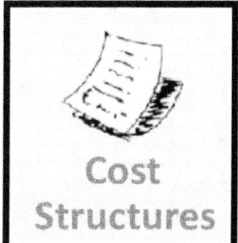

Your cost structure as it relates to the Business Model Canvas is closely related to your value proposition. At its highest level, cost structures are either cost or value focused.

Cost driven structures are focused on keeping costs or expenses down. Value driven structures are focused on providing more value or more revenue through premium offerings or services.

Companies that embrace a **cost driven** structure use automation or outsourcing to keep internal costs low, often resulting in competitive pricing. Operational excellence is often at the core of the business model of cost drive structures and are exemplified by WalMart and McDonalds. Because margins are small, business that are cost focused have to rely on volume to achieve satisfactory returns.

Companies that embrace a **value driven** structure use customer intimacy and high end components to create premium products. Customers that buy value driven products and services are less price conscious and value quality, performance, and convenience over price. Nordstrom and Rolex are examples of companies that have value driven structures.

Another element of a company's cost structure is the ratio

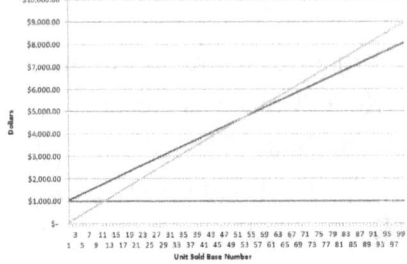

of fixed to variable costs they have. High variable costs relative to fixed costs have less upside reward, but also less downside risk.

By contrast, low variable costs relative to higher fixed costs have high upside rewards, but have substantially higher downside risk if break even volumes are not reached.

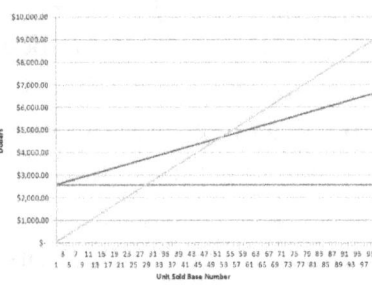

When considering cost structures, you should consider what are the most important costs that need more attention and which have less impact on the quality of your product or service. Also, consider which key resources and activities are most expensive and whether you benefit from moving up or down the value chain.

Do you understand your cost structures?

Environmental Forces

When you have completed the 9 blocks of the Business Model Canvas, you may have a well thought out business model. However, will it stand up in the real world? In the real world, your business will compete for market share and fight for survival every day.

For the most part, the 9 blocks that make up the Business Model Canvas discussion are elements that are within your control. At this point, however, we need to consider the opportunities and threats that are outside your control. Just because you can not control these elements does not mean that you should not account for them. While the 9 blocks generally comprise most discussions related to the Business Model Canvas, it is time to map out the outside environmental forces to get a more holistic view.

Key Trends

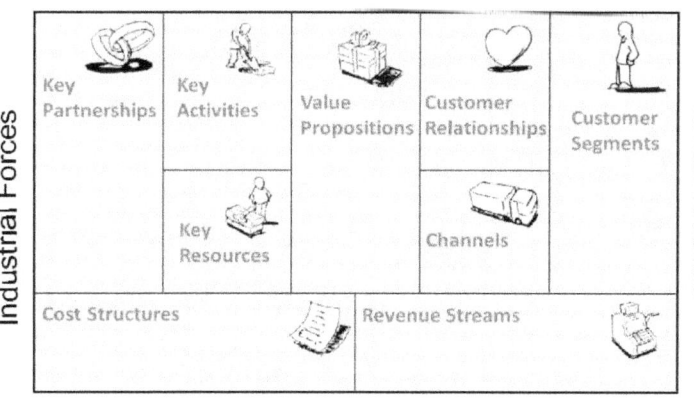

Macroeconomic Forces

By seeing the entire picture, you will gain deeper insight that you can then use to improve your business model.

Once you have what you think is the best business model, it is time to look at market forces, key trends, industry forces, and macroeconomic forces that will affect your business model. One thing that makes the environmental forces analysis different from the 9 blocks typically associated with the Business Model Canvas is that environmental forces are constantly changing and evolving, which requires a continuous effort on your part to reflect upon how they may affect each of your Business Model Canvas blocks.

Is your Business Model Canvas ready to incorporate its environmental forces?

Market Forces

The first environmental forces block is related to the market forces of the customer segments in your Business Model Canvas. The purpose of the "Market Forces" block is to verify that your model is in line with the evolving needs of your chosen customer segment.

When you are looking at market forces, you should start by asking, "Can I break down the customer segment further using demographic and psychographic data?" If your market segment relates to individual consumers (B2C), a tool called BusinessDecisions by Civic Technologies (available at many libraries) can help break down the customers into one of 65 consumer archetypes know a a "tapestry segments" in BusinessDecisions. A copy of the BusinessDecisions Tapestry Data Manual can be found under the resource tab of SteveBizBlog.com.

If your customer segment is a business (B2B), you can use a list of NAICS codes to consider alternative customer segments.

After you create a list of potential customer segments;
- Are there some segments that are more aligned with your business model?
- Do some have greater potential for higher profits margins?

Next, take a look at your list and determine which segments are most likely to grow and which are most likely to shrink. Harry Dent is an economist that looks at age and buying habits to assess the health of various consumer segments (B2C). A copy of Harry Dent's demand curves can be found under the resource tab of SteveBizBlog.com.

Next, you should look at what the specific customer segments really want and what will they likely resist. For example, if you are appealing to an older crowed, is it wise to develop a mobile app since may resist buying a smart phone?

Finally, it is time to consider if they really like your product or service better than other options and if there are customer switching costs you have to mitigate in your business model to finally get these customers to switch. For example, Sprint offers to buyout your existing contract if you agree to switch to their phone service as a way to mitigate switching costs. Also, commercial landlords often offer one or more months of free rent to compensate the customer expenses of relocating their business.

What are the market forces affecting your Business Model Canvas?

Critical Thinking About Market Forces

When completing a Business Model Canvas, it is helpful to guide the discussion through the use of questions. When it comes to looking at market forces that will affect your business model, the following set of questions should help you in thinking more critically about your business model. These questions are broken down into five categories: market issues, market segments, needs and demands, switching costs, and revenue attractiveness.

Market Issues:
- What are the critical issues affecting the customer landscape?
- What market shifts are underway?
- Where is the market heading?

Market Segments:
- Can you define the customer segment further by demographic and psychographic characteristics?
- Are there specific customer market segments that are growing or shrinking?
- Are there peripheral customer market segments that deserve more attention?

Needs & Demands:
- What are the customer's biggest expressed/unexpressed needs?
- What are the biggest unsatisfied customer needs?
- Where is demand increasing/decreasing?

Switching Costs:

- What binds the customer to a company and its offerings?
- What switching costs prevent customers from defecting to competitors?
- Is it easy for customers to find and purchase similar offers?
- How recognized and important is your brand?

Revenue Attractiveness:
- What are customers willing to pay for?
- Where can the largest margins be achieved?
- Can customers find and purchase cheaper products/services?

What market forces affect your business model?

Key Trends

The next environmental forces block is related to key trends. The "Key Trends" block is used to evaluate if your Business Model Canvas takes advantage of emerging market trends.

Are there any new technologies on the horizon that may undercut your business model? Don't just look at the advances in your industry that may affect your canvas. Disruptive technologies often come from other industries. For example, the rise of the internet replaced the role of travel agents since anyone could now search, compare, and purchase tickets online. Moreover, when cell phones became ubiquitous, many people began using their cell phone to check the time, displacing wristwatches.

Sometimes you have look at key trends outside your industry in addition to the advances within your industry.

Nokia was well ahead of the curve when it came to how cell phones would be used. They foresaw such things as the emergence of text messaging by observing how kids used their phones.

On the flip side, are their disruptive technologies that may supercharge your business model? For example, the McDonald brothers saw that increased car ownership would create a demand for the carhop restaurant.

Another key trend is regulatory changes. When the President signed the JOBS act in 2012, it changed the general solicitation rules. Changing the solicitation rules had a profound impact on my oil and gas investors education business since oil and gas producers could now advertise in ways previously prohibited.

Finally, you need to assess how society is changing. In "Next: The Future Just Happened," Michael Lewis looks at how the internet has changed the social fabric and our attitudes. For example, consider how Facebook or LinkedIn have changed how we interact with our friends and the way we work with others.

What are the key trends that will affect your Business Model Canvas?

Critical Thinking About Key Trends

When completing a Business Model Canvas, it is helpful to guide the discussion through the use of questions. When it comes to looking at key trends that will affect your business model, the following set of questions should help you in thinking more critically about your business model. These questions are broken into four trends: technology, regulatory, social and cultural, and socioeconomic.

Technology Trends:
- What are the major technological trends inside/outside your market?
- Which technologies represent opportunities/threats?
- Are there emerging peripheral trends that could affect your market?
- Which emerging technologies are peripheral customers adopting?

Regulatory Trends:
- Are there new or upcoming regulations that will influence your market?
- Are there current or new regulations/taxes that will affect customer demand?

Social & Cultural Trends:
- What are the key demographic/psychographic trends?
- What is the wealth distribution in your market?
- Are there sufficient disposable/discretionary income levels to support buying your product/service?

- What are your customer's spending patterns and are they changing?
- What affect does the customer's location (city, country) play?

Socioeconomic Trends:
- Are there shifts in cultural and social values that could affect your market?
- What trends might influence buyer behaviors?

What key trends affect your business model?

Industry Forces

The next environmental forces block is "Industry Forces" and this section is used to determine if your business model will have a competitive edge today and tomorrow.

To understand industrial forces, you need to asses who your competitors are. A tool called ReferenceUSA (available at many libraries) is a valuable tool to locate and assess your competition.

The SBA also has a tool called SizeUp that helps you to assess your competition.

After you generate a list of competitors, you will need to understand exactly what their business model provides.

Is there a dominant player in the industry? If so, you need to determine if they have the ability to marginalize or even crush your business if they see you are a threat.

Do they have a weakness that you can exploit? For example, Uber used a mobile app to create a peer-to-peer ride sharing model that companies like Yellow Cab could not compete with.

Do you have a process or technology that might disrupt these big companies?

Another question to ask yourself is how dependent are you on your key partners and suppliers? What would happen if they left or were not able to evolve with you?

Essentially when it comes to industry forces, you are performing a <u>SWOT analysis</u>. SWOT stands for Strengths, Weaknesses, Opportunity, and Threats as they relate to your industry position. Much literature has been published on SWOT and will serve as valuable resources for understanding your industrial forces.

What are the industry forces that will affect your Business Model Canvas?

Critical Thinking About Industry Forces

When completing a Business Model Canvas, it is helpful to guide the discussion through the use of questions. When it comes to looking at industry forces that will affect your business model, the following set of questions should help you in thinking more critically about your business model. These questions are broken into three categories: competitors, new entrants, and substitute products and services.

Competitors:
- Who are your key competitors?
- Who are the dominant players?
- What are their competitive advantages?
- What customer segments are they focused on?
- What are their cost structures?
- Can they exert influence on your margins?
- Are your competitors expanding or fading?

New Entrants:
- Are value chain companies expanding into your space?
- How are they different?
- What barriers do they need to overcome?
- Do they have a different value proposition?

Substitute Products and Services:
- Which products/services could replace yours?
- How much do they cost compared to yours?

- How easy/hard is it for customers to switch to substitutes?

What industry trends affect your business model?

Macroeconomic Forces

The next and final environmental forces block is "Macroeconomic Forces." This section is used to determine if your business model can adjust to macroeconomic shifts.

This is where keeping up with current events is important. In addition to watching world and local news programs each day, I use an internet news aggregator that searches various news sources and delivers the headlines in a single web page.

I generally reserve 1 hour every day to understanding the macroeconomic forces affecting my industries.

If you are short on time, the publication "The Week" is an excellent source that takes world and national current events and boils them down to their raw essences in a weekly magazine that is available in print and online.

Essentially when it comes to macroeconomic forces, we are looking at local, national, and world events that will affect our business model. As an example, I purchased a few properties in Gloucester County, VA a few years ago. I made this purchase after a new bridge was built to connect the Middle Peninsula to the industrial hub located on the Virginia Peninsula. The Virginia Peninsula is the home of the industrial shipyards of Newport News and many government offices. Prior to the new bridge, property on the Middle Peninsular was far less accessible to centers of employment which decreased property values.

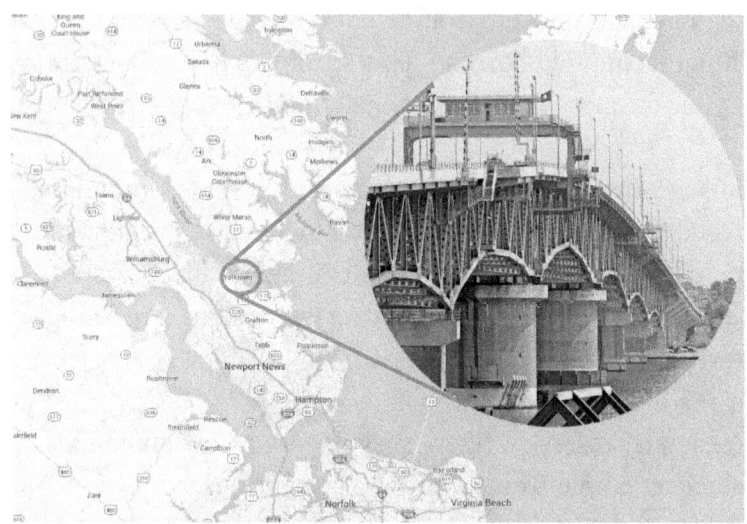

With the new bridge, property values rose on the Middle Peninsula at nearly 20% per year until an equilibrium was finally reached. By recognizing the effects that the bridge would have on local property values on the Middle Peninsula, I bought property early and made a lot of money that I wound not have if had I not seen how local macroeconomic conditions would change property values.

In addition to current events, you need to assess how global, national, and local economic trends will affect your business model. For example, have you factored in how the slowing Chinese economy or oil prices will affect your business model?

What about changing infrastructure? How did the interstate

highways system affect the automobile industry? What if there were more charging stations for electric cars?

Finally, how might access to capital such as crowd funding, or changing lending practices, or rising interest rates affect your business?

What are the macroeconomic forces that will affect your Business Model Canvas?

Critical Thinking About Macroeconomic Forces

When completing a Business Model Canvas, it is helpful to guide the discussion through the use of questions. When it comes to looking at macroeconomic forces that will affect your business model, the following set of questions should help you in thinking more critically about your business model. These questions are broken into four categories: market conditions, capital markets, commodity and other resources, and economic infrastructure.

Market Conditions:
- Is the economy in a boom or bust phase and what affect will it have on your model?
- What is happening in global and local economies that can effect your model?
- What is the unemployment rate now and going forward and will it affect your model?

Capital Markets:
- What is the state of capital markets and its affect on your model?
- How easy is it to obtain funding in your market segment?
- Is seed capital available?
- How costly is it to procure funds?

Commodities & Other Resources:
- What is the current and expected future status of commodity markets (e.g., oil, labor, and raw

materials) and will it affect your model?

- How easy/hard will it be to obtain necessary resources?
- How costly are they?
- What directions are prices headed?

Economic Infrastructure:

- What is the status of the infrastructure in your market?
- What is the status of transportation, trade, talent base, and access to suppliers/customers?
- Are individual and corporate tax rates conducive to your model?
- What is the state of the public services and organizations you will be dealing with?
- What is the quality of life and its affect on your model?

What macroeconomic trends affect your business model?

Coming Up with New Ideas

The task of generating new ideas through the business model canvas exercise should not be left to creative thinkers alone. Moreover, you should not only assemble a team of experts, but instead assemble a team of diverse individuals. To increase your team's diversity, include:

- People from various business units
- People of different ages
- People with different areas of expertise
- People with various levels of seniority
- People who have different backgrounds
- People from a variety of cultures

What does your creative team look like?

Inside Out Business Model

Ignore the status quo and don't build a better mousetrap. Stop focusing on what your competitors do. Instead, challenge orthodoxies. To do so, start with any of the nine business model building blocks and build outwards. While we typically start with customer segments to build a customer driven business model, there are four common starting points. The four most common starting points include:

1. **Resource Driven** - Innovation originates from an organization's existing infrastructure or through its partnerships to expand or transform the business model. For example, Amazon's web services were built on top of its retail infrastructure to offer data storage to other companies.

2. **Offer Driven** - Innovation originates by creating a new and unique value proposition that affects the other building blocks in new ways. For example, FedEx offered 24-hour package delivery guaranteed

3. **Customer Driven** - Innovation originates based on customer needs, access, or increased convenience that affect the other blocks in new ways. For example, 1-800-Got-Junk made trash-hauling not only more convenient, but through recycling and donation changed the industry's image.

4. **Financially Driven** - Innovation originates from new revenue streams, pricing mechanisms, or reduces cost structures that affect the other blocks in new ways. For example, Xerox leased copiers as opposed to forcing users to buy them.

Where will you start when you apply the Business Model Canvas to your business?

Red Ocean vs. Blue Ocean Strategy

Coined by W. Chan Kim and Renée Mauborgne, the term "red ocean" refers to all the industries in existence today, otherwise known as "the known market space." In red oceans, industry boundaries are defined and accepted and the competitive rules of the game are known. Companies try to outperform their rivals to grab a greater share of product or service demand. As the market space gets crowded, prospects for profits and growth are reduced. Products and services become commodities and cutthroat competition turns the ocean bloody. Hence, the term "red oceans."

Kim and Mauborgne suggest an alternate approach, which they call "blue ocean."

Blue oceans, by contrast, denote all the industries not in existence today, otherwise known as "the unknown market space." The unknown market space is untainted by competition. In blue oceans, demand is created rather than fought over. There is ample opportunity for growth that is both profitable and rapid. In blue oceans, competition is irrelevant because the rules of the game are waiting to be set. The term "blue ocean" is an analogy to describe the wider, deeper potential of market space that is not yet explored.

They suggest that companies can succeed not by battling competitors, but rather by creating "blue oceans" of uncontested market space. They assert that these strategic moves create a leap in value for the company, its buyers, and its employees while unlocking new demand and making the competition irrelevant. The strategic move must raise and create value for the market while simultaneously reducing features or services that are less valued by the current or future market.

Therefore, the blue ocean strategy begins by looking at your business to determine what you can eliminate or reduce to create better cost savings. Then you see what you can create or increase to get higher margins.

Cirque de Soleil is a good example. The founders looked at the traditional circus model and asked, "What if we eliminated animals, traveling from city to city, and reduced the fun factor as part of our value proposition? In exchange, we'll create more thrill and a higher danger factor in conjunction with a theme and increased reliance on artistic music and dance." The result was their customer segment no longer focused on families with kids and instead focused on theater goers. Not only did they save on the cost of animal care and the cost of star performers, they were able to charge more than double the ticket price of the traditional circus, creating much greater margins.

In another example of blue ocean thinking, the Nintendo Wii team looked at the traditional game console that relied on leading edge power and performance as the key to their value proposition. They asked, "What if we eliminated the high-end and costly game console that requires subsidies and reduced the focus on hardcore gamers? Instead, we'll create a new game controller with motion sensing and create more of a fun factor." This changed the customer segment from hardcore gamers to casual and family gamers. The result was Nintendo saved on the subsidies cost required to sell the traditional gaming systems and actually profited on the sales of the consoles. Furthermore, they were still able to collect royalties from game developers.

Can you apply a blue ocean strategy to your business?

Applying the Blue Ocean Strategy to the Business Model Canvas

To apply the Blue Ocean Strategy, you start with a Business Model Canvas that describes your industry and then look at your the business model canvas from three different perspectives: the cost prospective, value proposition, and the customer segment.

From the cost prospective, identify the highest cost infrastructure elements and see what would happen to the model if you eliminated or reduced them. Then consider the infrastructure investments you could make or improve upon and see what would happen to the model. When it comes to looking at your model from the cost prospective, ask yourself the following questions:

- What activities, resources, and partnerships have the highest cost?
- What happens if you reduce or eliminate some of these cost factors?
- How could you replace useless or costly elements by reducing expensive resources, activities, or partnerships?
- What value would be created by planning new investments?
- How will changes made from a cost prospective affect your value proposition and customer side of the model?

Next, look at your business model from the value proposition prospective and see what new value you can create or increase. Then see what value you can eliminate or reduce. When it comes to looking at your model from a value proposition prospective, ask yourself the following questions:

- What less valuable features or services could be eliminated or reduced?
- What features or services could be enhanced or created to produce a valuable new customer experience?
- What are the cost implications of your changes to your value proposition?
- How will changes to the value proposition affect the customer side of the model?

Finally, look at your business model from the customer prospective and see what new customer segments you could focus on. Then see what customer segments you can eliminate or reduce. When it comes to looking at your model from the customer prospective, ask yourself the following questions:

- Which new customer segments could you focus on and which segments could you possibly reduce or eliminate?

- What jobs do new customer segments really want to have done?
- How do the customers prefer to be reached and what kind of relationship do they expect?
- What are the cost implications of serving new customer segments?
- What effects does adding or eliminating customer segments have on your value proposition?

How would you start to apply the blue ocean strategy to your business?

www.ingramcontent.com/pod-product-compliance
Lightning Source LLC
Chambersburg PA
CBHW060403190526
45169CB00002B/725